WINGS

by Melanie Mitchell

first step nonfiction

Lerner Publications Company · Minneapolis

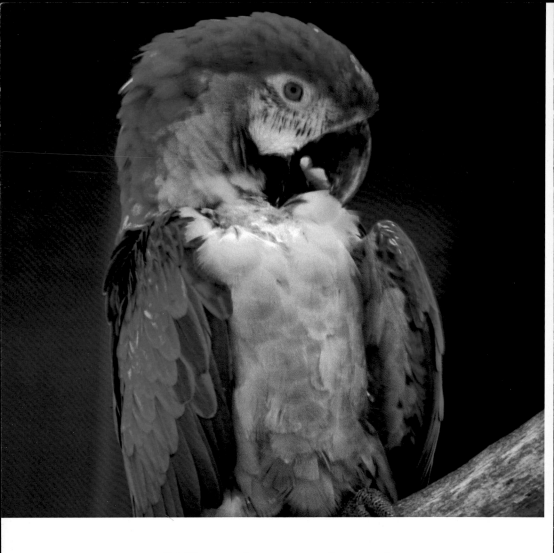

Who has wings?

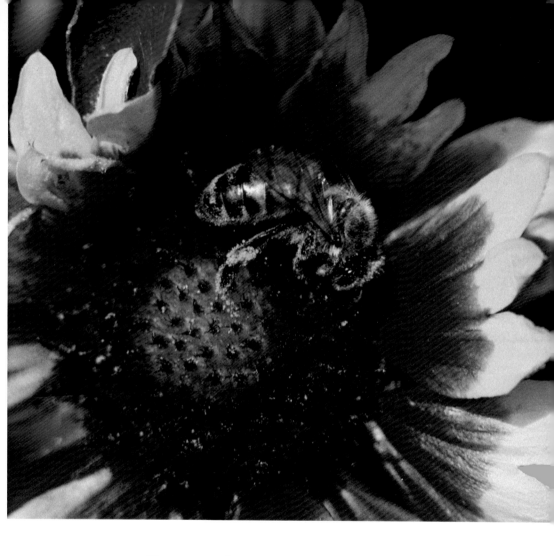

Bees have wings.

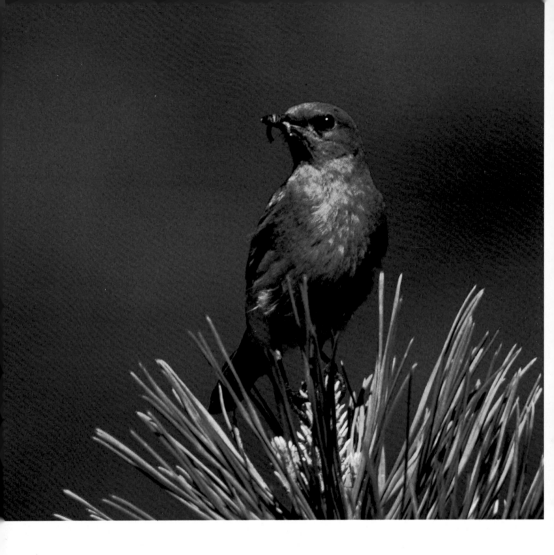

Bluebirds have wings.

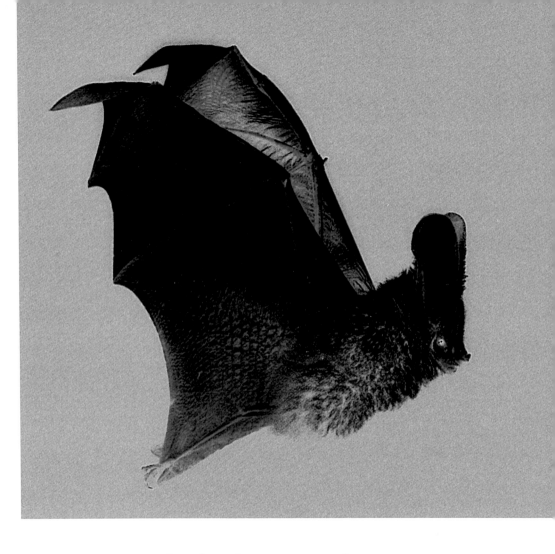

Bats have wings.

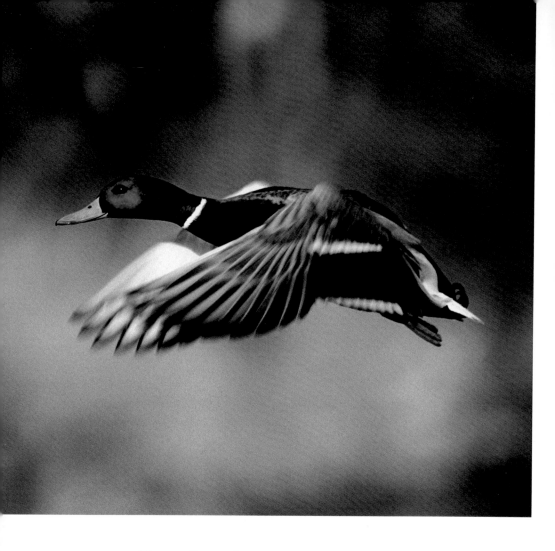

Ducks have wings.

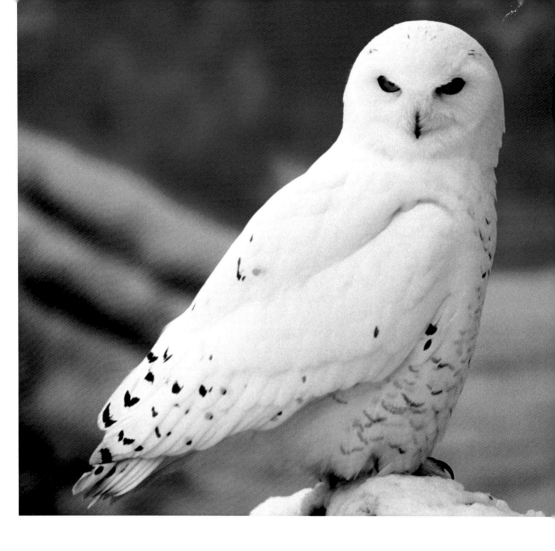

Owls have wings.

Animals fly with wings!